AF875910

TEACHER'S MANUAL AND ANSWER KEY

DEVELOPING CRITICAL READING SKILLS GRADE 4

Created and developed for Hayes School Publishing Co., Inc.
by Contemporary CPI Perspectives, Inc.

ANSWER KEY—PULL TO REMOVE

NO. BR622

TABLE OF CONTENTS

ANSWER KEY—PULL TO REMOVE

Some material in the following lessons has been adapted from the books indicated: Lessons 1 and 16, *Wonders of the Human Brain*; Lessons 3, 6, 8, and 22, *They Refused to Die*; Lessons 4 and 18, *Mindblowers*; Lesson 7, *Strange Creatures of the Desert*; all copyright 1982 by Contemporary Perspectives, Inc.; Lesson 2, *The First American Circus Ever*; Lessons 9 and 18, *The First Wild West Rodeo*, both copyright 1978 by Contemporary Perspectives, Inc.

ANSWER KEY

This Teacher's Manual has been prepared for the exclusive use of the teacher and is not supplied to pupils at any time.

Pages 2-3. Finding the Main Idea

Part A: 1. detail **2.** detail **3.** detail **4.** main idea

Part B: Main Idea 1; Details 2, 4, 6, 7

Pages 4-5. Remembering Sequence of Events

Part A: 5, 1, 4, 3, 2

Part B: 5, 4, 1, 3, 2

Part C: 4, 2, 5, 1, 6, 3

Part D: 1. False **2.** False

Pages 6-7. Understanding Cause and Effect

Part A:

1. Effect: The boys could not see anything.
Cause: It was snowing, and there was a heavy fog.

2. Cause: The boys were slowed by the storm.
Effect: The boys started to go down very carefully.

Part B:

1. Effect: Gary suggested that they head west.
Cause: Matt knew they were not going in the right direction.

2. Cause: The boys lost their balance.
Effect: They slipped into a hole up to their chests.

Part C:

1. Effect: Each of the boys had lost almost 30 pounds.
Cause: They didn't have enough food left.

2. Cause: They were too weak.
Effect: They would not be able to build another cave.

ANSWER KEY—PULL TO REMOVE

Pages 8-9. Fact and Opinion

Part A: 1. O **2.** O **3.** F **4.** O **5.** F **6.** F

Part B: Write the facts in the story.

1. Many ships disappear in storms at sea.
2. A few days after the ship first sailed, the captain died.
3. In 1872, another captain sailed with his family and seven sailors.
4. A month later, the ship was found.

Write the opinions in the story.

1. The *Mary Celeste* seemed to be under an evil spell from the start.
2. The sailors should not have gone on without him.
3. It was a bad idea to sail on this boat.
4. Only ghosts remained on board the ship!

Pages 10-11. Predicting Outcomes

Part A: 1. a **2.** a

Part B: Answers will vary but should include the idea that Juan will probably use the direction of the setting sun to find his way home.

Pages 12-13. Drawing Conclusions

Part A: **1.** b **2.** c

Part B: Answers will vary but should show an ability to argue convincingly on the basis of the facts presented.

Pages 14-15. Context Clues

Part A: **1.** c **2.** b **3.** a **4.** b **5.** a

Part B: **1.** d **2.** c

Pages 16-17. Setting

Part A: 1, 2, 4, 6, 7, 10

Part B: Students should write sentences 1, 2, 5, and 8 on the lines.

Part C: Answers will vary.

Pages 18-19. Character

Part A: 3, 4, and 7

Part B: Answers will vary but should include things like he's probably lonely, doesn't like people, likes to stick to a routine, etc.

Part C: Answers will vary.

Pages 20-21. Figurative Language: Similes

Part A: **1.** b **2.** b **3.** c

Part B: **1.** as slow as a snail **2.** the water seemed like glue; swimming like a fish **3.** I was braver than my pet kitten.

Part C: Answers will vary.

Pages 22-23. Synonyms

Part A: **1.** capture **2.** final **3.** entire **4.** joyful **5.** small **6.** twist **7.** expensive **8.** frighten **9.** caution **10.** straight

Part B: **1.** talking-speaking **2.** ridiculous-silly **3.** around-near **4.** maintain-think **5.** admire-like

Pages 24-25. Author's Purpose

Part A: **1.** a **2.** c **3.** b **4.** b **5.** b

Part B: to inform

Part C: Answer will vary.

Pages 26-27. Base Words: Adding -ing to Words Ending in e

Part A: **1.** living **2.** riding **3.** facing **4.** boring **5.** chasing **6.** holing **7.** deciding **8.** rising

Part B: **1.** ice **2.** bake **3.** bribe **4.** place **5.** take **6.** core

Part C: **1.** making **2.** like **3.** having **4.** take

Pages 28-29. Resolutions

Part A: **1.** Sam's sister, Sally, won the game for us that day. **2.** A little girl smiled at them and said, "Have you seen my cat?"

Part B: Answers will vary.

Pages 30-31. Exaggeration

Part A: 1, 3, 5, 7, and 10

Part B: Answers will vary.

Part C: Answers will vary.

DEVELOPING

CRITICAL READING

SKILLS

GRADE 4

Created and developed for Hayes School Publishing Co., Inc.
by Contemporary CPI Perspectives, Inc.

NO. BR622

Some material in the following lessons has been adapted from the books indicated: Lessons 1 and 16, *Wonders of the Human Brain;* Lessons 3, 6, 8, and 22, *They Refused to Die;* Lessons 4 and 18, *Mindblowers;* Lesson 7, *Strange Creatures of the Desert;* all copyright 1982 by Contemporary Perspectives, Inc.; Lesson 2, *The First American Circus Ever;* Lessons 9 and 18, *The First Wild West Rodeo,* both copyright 1978 by Contemporary Perspectives, Inc.

Finding the Main Idea

Find the main idea and the details in the stories below. Follow the directions. Remember that the **main idea** is the most important point the writer is trying to make. **Details** tell you more about the main idea.

A. Put an "X" on the line in front of the sentence with the main idea. Put a "✓" on the line in front of the sentences with details.

_____ 1. Memory helps us keep names, dates, and telephone numbers.

_____ 2. It is also the way we bring together and record everything we learn.

_____ 3. Memories are kept in the cells of the brain.

_____ 4. Memory is probably the most important part of the human mind.

B. Find **one** sentence with the main idea, and **four** sentences that give details about the main idea. Write them on the lines on page 3.

1. Scientists have found two types of memory in the human brain.
2. One is called short-term memory.
3. Scientists often wear long white coats.
4. The other is called long-term memory.
5. The brain keeps working even while we sleep.
6. Short-term memory helps us remember telephone numbers.
7. Long-term memory helps us to study and remember what we learn.
8. Sometimes scientists forget things, too.

Main Idea Sentence:

____

____

____

Detail Sentences:

1. ______________________________

____

____

2. ______________________________

____

____

3. ______________________________

____

____

4. ______________________________

____

____

Remembering Sequence of Events

In a story things or events happen in order, one after another. This order is called the sequence of events. Words such as **first**, **second**, **next**, **finally**, and **last** can help tell you the sequence of events.

In a well-written story, the sequence of events is organized very carefully. If you pay attention to the sequence of events, it will help you understand how and why things happen in the story.

The sentences of the stories below are not in correct order. Write the numbers in the correct sequence so the stories make sense.

A.

_____ Finally, the tightrope walker climbed the ladder.

_____ First the clowns put up two tall poles apart from each other.

_____ As he bowed, a clown placed a thin ladder against the poles.

_____ Then the tightrope walker bowed.

_____ Next they stretched a rope tight between the tops of the poles.

B.

_____ Once again, the cheers almost lifted the roof.

_____ To the wonder of all the people, he put the chair on the rope.

_____ First the Italian was handed a chair and a book.

_____ Then he sat on the chair with his legs up, reading.

_____ Next he carried the chair and book to the center of the rope.

C.

_____ As he was dancing, he slipped!

_____ When he reached the top, he stepped out on the rope.

_____ At the last second, he caught the rope with one hand.

_____ The tightrope walker climbed quickly.

_____ Finally, he waved at everyone to show he was all right.

_____ Then, he started to dance on the rope.

D. The sentences below are about the stories you have just read. Read each sentence and decide whether it is true or false. Circle the answer you have decided on.

1. The tightrope walker waved before he started to dance on the rope.

True False

2. The tightrope walker danced after he slipped.

True False

Understanding Cause and Effect

You know that the events in a story usually happen for a reason. This is called **cause and effect**. The reason the events happen is the cause, and the thing that happens is the effect.

Understanding cause and effect in a story can help you see why a character acts a certain way. It can also help you understand why certain things happen in a story.

Read each story below. Then fill in each missing cause or effect.

A. When they walked out of the cave, they could not see anything. A snowstorm and heavy fog made climbing impossible. Now there was great danger on Mount Hood. The safest thing to do was to return to the lodge. Slowed by the storm, the boys started to get back down very carefully.

1. Effect: The boys could not see anything.

   Cause: ______________________________

   ____

   ____

2. Cause: The boys were slowed by the storm.

Effect: ______________________________

____

____

B. The boys lost their balance. They slipped into a hole up to their chests. Matt knew they were not going in the right direction. Gary suggested, "We'd better head west."

1. Effect: Gary suggested that they head west.

Cause: ______________________________

____

____

2. Cause: The boys lost their balance.

Effect: ______________________________

____

____

C. Then disaster struck again. Their new snow home caved in. Each of the boys had lost almost 30 pounds. They didn't have enough food left. They would not be able to build another cave. They were too weak.

1. Effect: Each of the boys had lost almost 30 pounds.

Cause: ______________________________

____

____

2. Cause: They were too weak.

Effect: ______________________________

____

____

Fact and Opinion

A **fact** is something that is known to be true. It can be proven. An **opinion** is what someone believes is true and cannot be proven. Opinions often show what a person feels about something.

Writers use facts and opinions to tell stories. As you read, you should be able to tell the difference between facts and opinions. The opinions are part of the writer's point of view. They will help you understand the writer's purpose.

A. Write "F" in front of the sentences that are facts. Write "O" in front of the sentences that are opinions.

_____ 1. You should always talk to your plants.

_____ 2. Plants have feelings just like people do.

_____ 3. Plants need sun and water to grow healthy and strong.

_____ 4. Plants get along better with animals than with people.

_____ 5. If you water a plant too much, it will die.

_____ 6. Some plants don't need as much light as others.

B. Find the facts and opinions in the story below.

Many ships disappear in storms at sea. The *Mary Celeste* seemed to be under an evil spell from the start. A few days after the ship first sailed, the captain died. The sailors should not have gone on without him. In 1872, another captain sailed with his family and seven sailors. It was a bad idea to sail on this boat. A month later, the ship was found. Only ghosts remained on board the ship!

Write the facts in the story.

1. ______________________________

____

2. ______________________________

____

3. ______________________________

____

4. ______________________________

____

Write the opinions in the story.

1. ______________________________

____

2. ______________________________

____

3. ______________________________

____

4. ______________________________

____

Predicting Outcomes

A writer often gives clues in a story to help you guess what will happen. This guessing is called **predicting outcomes**. Sometimes the clues are about the characters in the story or about the sequence of events.

As you read, look for these clues. They can help you predict what a character might do and how the story might end.

A. Read the stories below. Then circle the letter of the sentence that tells what probably happened.

1. The raccoon came out only at night. He didn't like being around people. He would knock over the garbage cans and eat whatever he found. One night we decided to hide in the branches of a tree. We waited a long time. Finally, we heard something coming. We turned on the flashlight to see. What we didn't know was that raccoons climb trees whenever they're scared.

a. The raccoon climbed the oak tree they were sitting in.

b. The raccoon ran away.

2. Sally was a stubborn girl. She was taking riding lessons. So far she had ridden a horse that only cantered or moved slowly. Sally wanted to make the horse gallop or run fast, but her teacher said she wasn't ready yet. Every day Sally would ask, "Am I ready yet?" Every day the teacher said, "Maybe next week, Sally." One day, the teacher was late, and Sally took her horse out alone.

a. Sally tried to make the horse gallop by herself.

b. Sally decided to wait until the teacher arrived.

B. Read the story below. Then write a sentence to tell what probably happened.

Juan liked to walk in the fields near his house. He knew his way and never got lost. But one day Juan lost track of time. He was watching a sheep and her baby lamb as they played together. When Juan looked up, he saw that the sun was about to set. He remembered what his father had told him. The sun always sets in the west.

What will happen? ______________________________

____

____

____

____

____

____

____

____

____

Drawing Conclusions

A **conclusion** is an idea or understanding you reach about something after adding up all the facts. For example: You know that the toaster does not pop up the toast, and you forget to keep an eye on the toaster. Then you smell smoke coming from the kitchen. You might draw the conclusion that the toaster burned your toast.

A writer does not always tell you everything. It may be left up to you to make or draw the conclusion. You can draw conclusions about characters as well as events. Drawing conclusions can be fun, as you put together clues given in the story.

A. Read the stories below. Draw a conclusion about the person or situation. Then circle the answer that you think best matches your conclusion.

1. Gary Schneider's father stared at the small empty car in the parking lot of the lodge. His 16-year-old son and two friends had left the lodge days ago. They were going to make a risky climb to the top of Mount Hood. The weather had become very bad, and their return was long overdue.

The three boys:

a. are probably having fun on the mountain.

b. are having trouble during the climb.

c. are climbing another mountain.

d. never left the lodge.

2. Justine grew up near the beach. Her family owned horses, and she loved to ride her horse along the water. When she got older, Justine started learning how to surf. But when she was 17, Justine's family moved to a big city in the midwest. There they lived in an apartment high up. They had to sell all the horses when they moved.

Justine:

a. made a lot of new friends.

b. loved living in the city.

c. missed her horse and the beach.

d. wanted a sister.

B. Read the story below. Then answer the question.

Loch Ness is a lake in Scotland. For 14 centuries, people have reported seeing a "monster" in the lake. Loch Ness is more than 700 feet deep in places. The water is dark and cold. It is a perfect place for a large water animal to hide. One scientist has said that the Loch Ness Monster may be a giant reptile. More and more people spot something in the lake every year.

Do you think the stories about the Loch Ness Monster are just made up? Explain your conclusion.

____

____

____

____

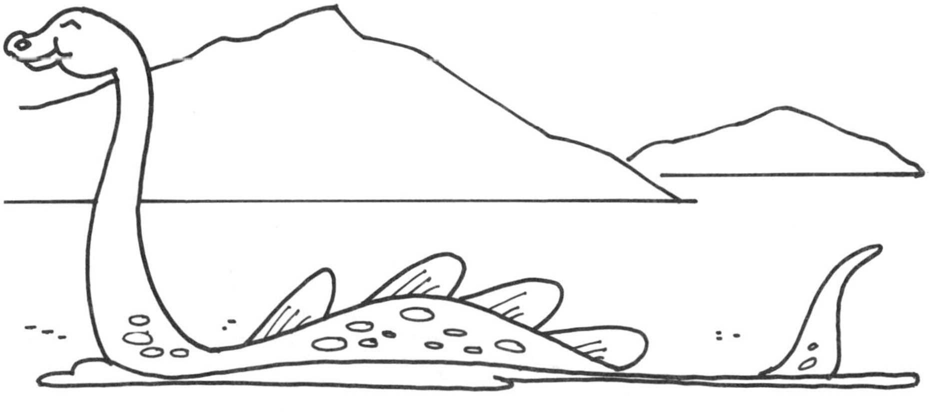

Context Clues

A **context** is the place or situation in which something is found. When you read, you may come across new words. The sentence you are reading is the context in which you find the new words. You often can find clues in the sentence to help you figure out the meaning of these words. These clues are called **context clues**.

Using context clues can be like putting together the pieces of a puzzle. The better you become at this skill, the more you will enjoy reading.

A. Read the passages below. Then circle the letter of the word that gives the meaning of the word in bold type.

1. In the **parched** desert, there is never much water for plants.

   a. pretty b. cold c. dry

2. All desert plants must be able to **survive** without water.

   a. drink b. live c. die

3. Some cactuses **provide** shelter for many kinds of animals.

   a. give b. take c. surprise

4. The spines of the cactus **discourage** animals from getting too close.

a. help b. stop c. send

5. Owls can rest **securely** in the side of the cactus.

a. safely b. painfully c. foolishly

B. The word in bold type in each sentence below is a made-up word. Circle the letter of the word that gives the meaning.

1. Maria and Rose both wanted to win the swimming race. They practiced hard every day. When Maria won, Rose was **faddle**. She shook hands with Maria, but she felt **faddle** all day.

The word **faddle** means:

a. fast

b. happy

c. calm

d. unhappy

2. James shouted as soon as he saw the car coming. When the car stopped, he called the little dog. After the dog was safe, Mrs. Jasper thanked James. With his **tully** thinking, James saved the dog's life.

The word **tully** means:

a. happy

b. sorry

c. quick

d. painful

Setting

As you read the stories below, watch for the setting. Remember that the **setting** is where and when the story takes place. A writer uses clues to tell you about the setting. Look for clues about the weather or the time of day. Stories can be set in the present, the past, or the future.

A. Circle the number of each sentence that tells about the setting.

1. They had to battle the sea all the time.
2. It was hard to keep the small boat from turning over.
3. They started to feel weaker every day.
4. They were just a dot on the Pacific Ocean.
5. They ate some turtle meat to stay alive.
6. On the 22nd day of the trip, there was a terrible storm.
7. Crashes of thunder scared them all.
8. Dougal learned how to catch fish.
9. He made a hook from a small nail.
10. The boat kept moving toward land.

B. Find the four sentences that are about the setting. Then write them on the lines below.

1. The airplane was caught in a terrible storm.
2. It crashed in the jungle of Peru.
3. At first, Julie didn't know what had happened.
4. "I'm lucky to be alive," she thought.
5. It was Christmas Eve, 1971.
6. Other people were probably sleeping peacefully.

7. Julie felt very scared.

8. She moved slowly and carefully through the jungle.

1. ______________________________

____

2. ______________________________

____

3. ______________________________

____

4. ______________________________

____

C. Write a sentence telling more about the setting of the plane crash in Peru. Use your imagination.

____

____

____

Character

Character is what a person is like. A writer uses details about character to make the people in a story seem real. The details might be about how the people feel or what they look like. They might be about how the people act and why they act that way.

If you know more about the people in a story, you can guess what they might do. You can compare them with yourself and with people you know.

A. Circle the number of each sentence that tells details about a person's character.

1. Many towns picked up the idea of the rodeo.
2. The rodeo became a real show.
3. Polly Lee loved being a trick rider.
4. She has always liked horses.
5. The rodeo went on even in the rain.
6. The mud made it dangerous to ride.
7. Bertha always wanted the wildest horse she could find.
8. The horse kicked and fussed a lot.

B. Read the story below. Watch for details about character.

Mr. Gibbons lived alone. He had never married. His house was on top of a hill. It was very old. The house was filled with old things his family had owned for a hundred years. No matter what, Mr. Gibbons always had tea at 4 o'clock. Sometimes, he would not answer the door when someone knocked.

What can you tell about the character of Mr. Gibbons?

C. Write a few sentences describing the character of someone you know. You can also make up a character of your own.

Figurative Language: Similes

Figurative language is language that compares one thing to something we would normally think of as very different. One kind of figurative language that does this is **simile**. Similes compare things by using the words "like," "as," or "than."

For example: Anna sang like a bird.

A. Read the sentences below. Then answer the questions. Circle the letter of the right answer.

1. Eric was the best basketball player in the class. He was as tall as a tree.

   What is Eric being compared to?

   a. a basketball player   b. a tree

2. The yellow house was brighter than the sun.

   What words make up the simile?

   a. the yellow house   b. brighter than the sun.

3. The snow on the hill looked like the icing on a cake.

   What is the snow being compared to?

   a. a hill   b. a cake   c. the icing on a cake

B. Read the following story. Then answer the questions.

It took me all summer to learn to swim. At first, I was as slow as a snail. The water seemed like glue, and I was stuck in it. At least I was braver than my pet kitten. By the end of the summer, I was swimming like a fish.

1. What is the simile that uses the word **as**?

____

____

____

2. What are the two similes that use the word **like**?

____

____

____

____

____

3. What simile uses the word **than**?

____

____

____

C. Write a sentence about yourself. Use a simile with the words **as**, **than**, or **like**.

____

____

____

____

Synonyms

Different words that mean almost the same thing are called **synonyms**. Writers use synonyms to make the way they tell a story more interesting.

When you talk to your friends, don't you try to vary the way you say things? Writers try to vary their writing in the same way.

A. Look at each word on the list below. Unscramble the letters next to it to find a synonym. Write it on the line.

1.	trap	turapec	________
2.	last	lifan	________
3.	whole	tereni	________
4.	happy	julyof	________
5.	tiny	lalms	________
6.	bend	switt	________
7.	costly	senixpeev	________
8.	scare	nethfirg	________
9.	warn	ocanuti	________
10.	level	grasthit	________

B. Use a synonym from the box for each word in bold type in the sentences below. Then rewrite the sentences.

like	silly	near	speaking	think

1. Some people believe that **talking** to plants helps them to grow better.
2. Others think it is **ridiculous** to talk to plants.

3. Do plants really know what is going on **around** them?
4. Some scientists **maintain** that plants are very sensitive.
5. People who **admire** the beauty of plants should treat them well.

1. ______________________________

____

2. ______________________________

____

3. ______________________________

____

4. ______________________________

____

5. ______________________________

____

Author's Purpose

A writer of a book is called an **author**. Someone's reason for doing something is called the **purpose**. So the reason someone writes a story is called the **author's purpose**. One purpose is to convince the reader of something. Other purposes are to teach, to inform, and to entertain. In the exercises below, look for the reason **why** someone would write these statements.

A. Read each sentence. Circle the letter of the correct author's purpose.

1. Children should always have pets when they are young.

   a. to convince

   b. to entertain

   c. to teach

2. There will be a concert at 8:00 on Saturday night.

   a. to entertain

   b. to convince

   c. to inform

3. There are many different ways to catch a fish.

   a. to entertain

   b. to teach

   c. to convince

4. The school will be closed tomorrow because of the holiday.

   a. to convince

   b. to inform

   c. to entertain

5. Once upon a time, there was a beautiful princess who lived in a tower.

    a. to inform

    b. to entertain

    c. to convince

B. Read the sentences below and then write the author's purpose.

If you like music, there are two school groups you can join. The first one is the school band. If you don't play an instrument, you can always join the chorus.

Author's Purpose:

____

C. Write a few sentences of your own that have the same author's purpose as the sentences above.

____

____

____

____

____

____

Base Words: Adding -ing to Words Ending in E

A **base word** is a word to which endings can be added. When writers add **ing** to words that end in **e**, they drop the **e**.

For example: give = giv + ing
giving

To find the base word, take off the **ing** and add **e**.

For example: giving = give + e
give

A. Add **ing** to each word in parentheses and write the new word on the line.

1. This summer I will be (live) with my grandparents.
   ____
2. I'll spend a lot of time (ride) their old horse Rosebud.
   ____
3. The house is (face) a mountain and a stream.
   ____
4. Jake is out back (bore) a hole in the fence.
   ____
5. You shouldn't waste time (chase) red foxes.
   ____
6. The outlaws have been (hole) up in the valley.
   ____
7. My sister is still (decide) whether or not to come.
   ____
8. I like (rise) early in the country.
   ____

B. Find the base word of each word in parentheses and write it in on the line.

1. Would you like to help me (icing) the cake?

   ____

2. We're also going to (baking) some pies and muffins.

   ____

3. He was arrested for trying to (bribing) a judge.

   ____

4. Paul will (placing) the pies near the window to cool.

   ____

5. (Taking) the apple pie with you when you go.

   ____

6. He didn't see why he should (coring) the apple.

   ____

C. Choose a word from the box to complete each sentence. Add **ing** if you need to. Write the word in the space.

take	have	make	like

1. I've been ______________________ plans for the picnic.
2. If you ______________________ parades, you should come.
3. We'll be ______________________ a cookout tonight, too.
4. Make sure you ______________________ your sweater with you.

Resolution

Most stories follow a plan. First the most important characters are introduced. Next the setting and plot are developed. Then there is usually one big event at the end of the story that solves a problem. This event is often called the **resolution**.

Sometimes the resolution is a surprise. When you read, look for clues to help you guess what might happen.

A. Read each story. Decide which sentence has the resolution in it. Then write it on the line below.

1. Everyone was looking forward to the basketball game on Saturday. It was supposed to start at 2:00. At 1:00 I got a phone call from Sam. He said he couldn't play, because he had the measles. I couldn't believe it. Sam was the star player! I called every boy I knew, but it was too late. Everyone had plans. Suddenly, I thought of one more person to try. I made the call, and this time I was lucky. Sam's sister, Sally, won the game for us that day!

____

____

2. Rosa and Lee had passed the old house many times. It was on their way to school. Every morning there was a milk bottle on the front step. And every afternoon, the milk bottle was gone. But the old house looked as if no one lived there. One rainy day, as they were passing the house, they heard a low moan come from inside. Lee started to run away, but Rosa said they should find out what it was. They went up to the door and knocked. There was no answer. Just then the door swung open, and Lee screamed. Something small and black ran past them. And then the door opened all the way. A little girl smiled at them and said, "Have you seen my cat?"

____

____

B. Read the story below. Then write a resolution for the story.

John's family went to the mountains to ski. John had never been skiing before, but he was sure he could do it better than anyone. After all, how hard could it be? You just put the skis on your feet and slide down a hill. Big deal! When John's father told him to start on the beginner's hill, John just laughed. He went to the hardest path he could find. Then he strapped on his skis and started down the mountain.

____

____

____

____

____

____

Exaggeration

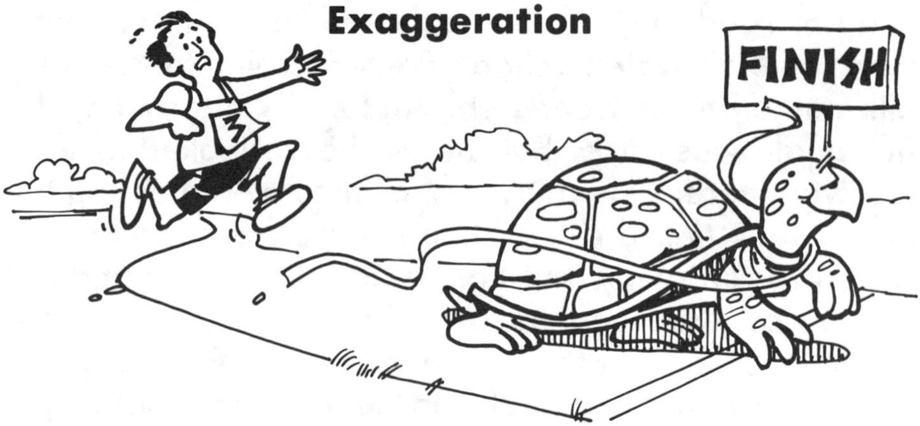

One tool a writer has to make a story better is **exaggeration**. You exaggerate when you take a quality something has and add to it. Sometimes this is done by comparing two things that have something in common, but are not really the same. For example: "Roger was as slow as a turtle." Roger is slow. So is a turtle. But you know that Roger could not really be "as slow as a turtle." This is an exaggeration.

Often, writers use exaggeration to make their readers laugh. Watch for exaggeration when you read. It is a clue that the story you are reading is funny.

A. Read the sentences. Then circle the number of each sentence that is an example of exaggeration.

1. It was so hot that you could fry an egg on the sidewalk.
2. The wind blew across the mountains at night.
3. Joe's stories were so full of holes you could walk through them.
4. There was not even room in the cabin for a desk and chair.
5. It will take forever and a day to finish this crossword puzzle.
6. In our house, we all take turns walking the dog.
7. Jill drove a car that was a block long.
8. The little old man was as wrinkled as a prune.

9. There are 50 new recipes for cooking vegetables in this book.

10. I promise I'll never laugh again as long as I live.

B. Read the story. Whenever you see a blank space, make up an exaggeration and write it on the lines below.

It was getting late. I was so hungry that ____________. My little brother made such a mess in the kitchen that ______________________. I knew my parents wouldn't be home until ______________________. I decided to make myself a meal ______________________.

1. ____

____

2. ____

____

3. ____

____

4. ____

____

C. Use the exaggerations below to write your own story.

— as flat as a board
— so happy, she could jump over the moon
— as tall as the Empire State Building

____

____

____

____

____

____

Run-On Lines

When a sentence is made up of two or more ideas but does not use proper punctuation, it is called a **run-on**. This is because the ideas have been run together. Careful writers usually do not write run-on sentences unless they are doing it for an effect.

To correct a run-on, you can break it into two separate sentences using correct punctuation. For example:

I have a new camera it is very easy to use.
I have a new camera. It is very easy to use.

Sometimes you can use a comma and words such as **and**, **or**, **so**, **because**, or **but** to connect the sentences. For example:

I like to go to the zoo I don't like the circus.
I like to go to the zoo, but I don't like the circus.

Notice that a comma is used before the word **but**.

Correct the run-on sentences below and write the new sentence or sentences on the lines.

1. The brain keeps working when you sleep it also keeps other parts of the body working.

____

____

____

2. When you sleep your heart beats more slowly your breathing becomes deeper.

____

____

____

3. In the first part of sleep the muscles relax it is not a very deep sleep.

4. Part two of sleep happens about 30 minutes later the sleeper falls into a deeper rest.

5. In part three the body becomes more relaxed blood pressure drops.

6. Part four is the deepest part it is difficult to wake the sleeper.

7. You dream about four or five times a night you probably do not remember all of your dreams.

Fables

One very old type of story is called a **fable**. The characters in fables are usually animals who act like people. Fables always have a lesson to teach about the right way to live or how to do something. This lesson is called a **moral**. The moral usually comes at the end of the fable. Morals are most often summed up in a single, short sentence. For example, the moral of one famous fable is "Slow but steady wins the race." This is the moral of *"The Tortoise and the Hare."*

Fables and their morals are about common human problems. Can you think of any other fables?

A. Read the fable below. Then circle the number of the best moral.

The Moth Who Wanted to See the World

There once was a baby moth who wanted to see the world. Mama Moth said, "All you have to do is spread your wings. The wind will catch you and carry you away." But Baby Moth was scared. She said the wind would stop blowing, and she would fall.

One day she saw a tall flower and decided to climb it. She thought that maybe now she would see the world. But all she could see was another flower.

Suddenly the wind started to blow. Baby Moth held on as tightly as she could, but the wind blew too hard. She quickly spread her wings and let go of the flower. The wind carried her away. "Now this is the way to see the world!" thought Baby Moth.

The moral is:

1. The world is too big for moths.
2. You never know what you can do until you try.
3. Insects with wings can go anywhere.

B. Read the fable below. Then write a moral of your own.

The Swan, the Rooster, and the Horse

A swan, a rooster and a horse lived together on a farm. "Don't you think I'm the most beautiful animal you have ever seen?" asked the swan. And the others said, "Yes, you are a very beautiful swan."

One day the horse said to the swan, "You must sound as beautiful as you look. Wake me when the sun rises." But when the swan called the next morning, what a loud, awful voice she had! The horse was not pleased. The rooster said nothing.

The next day, when the sun rose, the rooster crowed, "Cocka-doodle-doo." The horse was very happy. When he saw the rooster, he said, "I want you to wake me every morning. You have the nicest voice on the farm."

The moral is: ______________________________

____

____

Paraphrasing

After you read a story, you may be asked what it was about. Telling a story in your own words is called **paraphrasing**.

As you read, pay attention to the most important points in the story. If it is a story about real people or science or history, try to remember the important information. If the story is fiction about people, think about the characters and what they did.

A. Read the stories below. Then circle the letter next to the best paraphrase.

1. Robert Earl Hughes was born in 1926 in Fish Hook, Illinois. He weighed 11½ pounds. When he was six years old, he weighed 203 pounds. At 10 he weighed 378. At the time of his death in 1958, he weighed 1,069 pounds. He was so large he had to be buried in a piano case.

a. Robert Earl Hughes was born in Fish Hook, Illinois, in 1926. He died in 1958.

b. Robert Earl Hughes was born a large baby in 1926. During his life, he gained huge amounts of weight. He weighed 1,069 pounds when he died in 1958.

c. Robert Earl Hughes weighed 203 pounds when he was six years old. He weighed 1,069 pounds when he died. He was born in Illinois.

2. I'll tell you about a tough rodeo contest that looks easy at first. Roping calves takes a lot of skill. The calves move at top speed. You have to chase after them trying to throw a rope over their heads. A calf is one of the trickiest animals I know. It can change direction, slow down, or speed up in a split second.

a. Rodeo contests may look easy, but they're very hard. Catching a calf is very tricky.

b. Rodeos are hard. You have to catch a calf. They run very fast.

c. There is a rodeo contest that takes a lot of skill. You have to rope a calf. Calves are fast, tricky, and hard to catch.

B. Read the following story. Then write your own paraphrase.

A park ranger in Virginia named Roy Sullivan has been struck by lightning seven times! It became such a problem that he would leave town if a storm was headed his way. Somehow, no matter what he did, he always managed to get hit anyway. Sullivan has had his hair catch on fire. He has even lost an eyebrow and a toenail from his run-ins with lightning. A few years ago, he had a dream that he had been struck for the last time. He has not been hit since.

Paraphrase:

____

____

____

____

____

Alliteration

When you read a story or a poem, you may notice that the sounds of some words are repeated. For example: The calm quiet ocean curled around our feet. Notice that three of the words — calm, quiet, and curled — begin with the same sound. They do not all start with the same letter.

Phrases in which two or more words begin with the same sound have **alliteration**. Poets often use alliteration to produce special sound effects in their writing. Alliteration can make language sound almost like music.

To find alliteration, read the lines to yourself. Listen for the sounds with which the words start. Remember that words can start with the same letter but have a different sound.

A. Read the sentences silently to yourself. Then circle the letter next to the list of words that have all the examples of alliteration in the sentence.

1. Susie sang the silly song in the center of the room.

   a. sang, silly, song
   b. Susie, sang, silly, song
   c. Susie, sang, silly, song, center

2. The basket of bluebells looked pretty in the bare room.

   a. pretty, room
   b. basket, bluebells, bare
   c. basket, bluebells

3. The newly knitted sweater was nice and warm.

   a. sweater, was, nice
   b. newly, nice
   c. newly, knitted, nice

4. The fiery flare of the flames was reflected in our faces.

   a. flames, was, faces
   b. fiery, flare, flames, faces
   c. fiery, flare, reflected

B. Use each of the phrases below in a sentence. Add more words with alliteration to each phrase if you can.

1. the best beach in Bermuda

____

____

2. a pair of pretty peacocks

____

____

3. a can of cooked cabbage

____

____

4. wet weather on Wednesday

____

____

Haiku

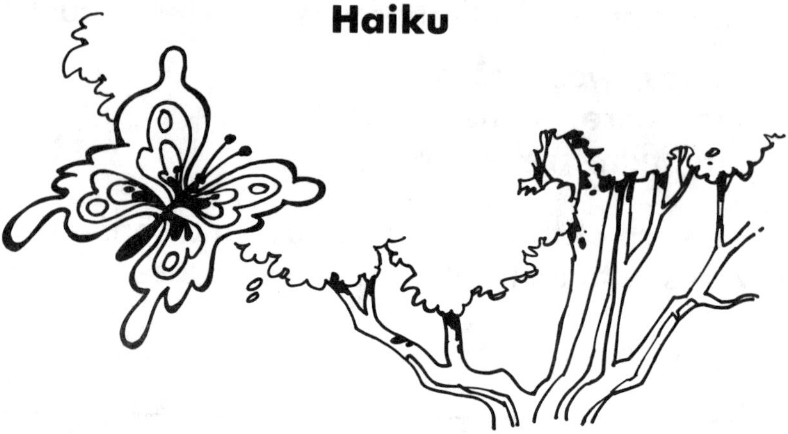

The haiku is a Japanese poem of 17 syllables in three lines. It gives an impression of a brief moment. The poem does not rhyme. For example:

The falling flower
I saw drift back to the branch
Was a butterfly.

Notice that the first word in each line is capitalized.

Writing a haiku is like piecing together a puzzle. You must think of an idea and stick with it. It is not easy to write a haiku, but it can be fun to try.

A. Read the first two lines of each haiku. Then try to write a third line of your own. Don't worry about the number of syllables, but make the line short.

1. My favorite month
   Comes in like a lion and

   ____

2. Softly the breeze blows:
   Far clouds draw apart, and for

   ____

3. Water in the lake
   Makes beautiful reflections

   ____

4. In the maple tree
An empty nest is hiding

____

5. Underneath the ground
The earthworms will be moving

____

6. A garden in June
Is full of green tomatoes

____

B. Write a haiku about each subject listed below.

1. Starting school in the fall

____

____

____

2. Traveling to a new place

____

____

____

3. The first snowfall of winter

____

____

____

4. Making a new friend

____

____

____

Suspense

In an adventure or mystery story, the writer tries to keep you interested to the very end. Sometimes a writer creates excitement by using **suspense**. Suspense is a feeling of fear and excitement created when you know that something is about to happen, but you aren't sure what. One old nickname for a suspenseful book or movie is a "cliff-hanger." Can you guess what this means?

Suspense is created in lots of different ways. Usually, there is an element of danger involved. One common way is to end a chapter when the main character is caught in a difficult situation. The writer can be sure that you'll keep reading to find out what happens next!

A. Read the sentences below. Circle the number of each sentence that creates suspense.

1. Just as Peter opened the door, all the lights went out.
2. The house they lived in was painted blue and green.
3. They could hear nothing except the heavy footsteps coming slowly up the stairs.
4. The room felt very hot and stuffy.

5. As they lost control of the boat, they knew they were heading straight for a waterfall.

6. In the forest all around them were beautiful plants and trees and birds.

7. In the summer months, the house was always full of shouting and laughter.

8. As she lost control of her skis she could hear people shouting behind her.

B. Read the stories below. Then write a suspenseful last sentence for each one.

1. When they had reached 9,000 feet, the three climbers decided to have some fun. On the side of the mountain, they built an eight foot square ice fort. It was large enough for them to stand in. They could even store supplies on the shelves they had built.

____

____

____

____

2. Just before Christmas, Anna's mother left the family home in the jungle of Peru. She picked up Anna at school in the city. Mother and daughter prepared to fly back to their home in the jungle. The weather reports were good, and they left on schedule.

____

____

____

____

Multiple Word Meanings

You know that some words have more than one meaning. When you read a story, you may find one of these words in a sentence. Usually you can tell which meaning is intended by looking at the rest of the sentence. For example:

If you drop a stone in the river, it will sink. **Sink** has two meanings. One is a noun meaning **a small tub that holds water**. The other is a verb meaning **to drop down**. You can see that the second meaning is the one meant here.

There are usually clues in a sentence to tell you what part of speech is meant.

A. Read the sentences below. Then circle the letter of the correct meaning for each word in bold type.

1. You can **skip** the first chapter if you've already read it.

   a. leave out b. leaping step

2. I'd like some of that **punch** if there's any left.

   a. a drink b. hit

3. You must **stick** to your original plans.

   a. piece of wood b. stay close

4. It won't be my fault if you **trip** over the last step.

   a. stumble b. travel far away

5. Are the **rest** of you coming with us?

   a. take it easy b. ones left over

6. Sometimes I **long** for a nice quiet family.

   a. measure of distance b. wish for

7. You should always keep your records in a **log**.

   a. account book b. wood

8. My father works for a **firm** of lawyers.

   a. company b. solid

B. Complete each sentence by using one of the words from Section A.

1. We are taking a ________________ to Washington, D.C. this year.
2. The president said, "Speak softly and carry a big ________________."
3. We'll need at least one ________________ to get the fire going.
4. I promise not to ________________ you if you tell me you don't like this dress.
5. Some runners ________________ with a jump rope when they work out.
6. After this week, I need a long ________________.
7. Is the ice ________________ enough to skate on?
8. The movie was so ________________ that I fell asleep in the middle.

Probability and Certainty

When you read a story, notice that the writer gives you certain clues to figure out what is happening and what is likely to happen later. Sometimes the writer lets you know that something is sure to happen. This is a **certainty**. When you can only guess at what will most likely happen, it is called a **probability**.

A. Read the following stories and the statements that follow them. Circle the letter next to the correct statements. There may be more than one for each story.

1. Celia's family spent every summer on Snow Island. This summer would be no different. They planned to leave on June 1, and stay for eight weeks. But in the third week of May, something happened. Celia fell off her bike and broke her leg.

a. Celia will definitely still go to Snow Island with her family.

b. Celia will probably not go to Snow Island with her family.

c. Celia will definitely have a different kind of summer this year.

2. It had been raining on and off for a week. When it seemed to stop for good, Gary and Scott ran outside to explore. Everything was soaking wet, but they didn't mind. The weather had been so hot that it felt good to cool off. Their uncle Ken shouted a warning as they moved further away from the house. "It's bound to start raining again, boys. Don't go too far away."

a. Gary and Scott will definitely get caught in a rainstorm.

b. Gary and Scott will probably be caught in another rainstorm.

c. Gary and Scott will definitely get wet whether it rains again or not.

B. Read the following statements about what will happen. Then write your own short story to match the statements.

Ellen will definitely find a way to earn the money she needs.

Ellen will probably have to work at more than one job after school to make the money.

Imagery In Poetry

The use of language in poetry can be different from the use of language in everyday speech. One kind of poetic language is called **imagery**. It is the use of special details to describe a particular person, place, idea, object, or event. For example: The baby's hand looked like a flower with tiny white petals.

Good imagery should help you to see, hear, or feel something in a new way.

A. Read the sentences below. Circle the number of each sentence that has imagery.

1. The peacock stood very close to the pond.
2. The town was covered by a blanket of clean, white snow.
3. Her anger flashed from her eyes like knives.
4. We raked all the old leaves into a pile.
5. The sea sparkled like glass.
6. No one knows where the alarm clock is.
7. We had a wonderful time at the beach.
8. The moon smiled down just for us.

B. For each item listed below, think of an image that describes it in a new way.

1. an empty house ______________________________
2. a red dress ______________________________
3. a football game ______________________________
4. a bookcase full of books ______________________________
5. a train ______________________________
6. a noisy classroom ______________________________

C. Choose one of your images from Part B, and write a short poem about it.

____

____

____

Pages 32-33. Run-on Lines

1. The brain keeps working when you sleep, and it also keeps other parts of the body working.
2. When you sleep your heart beats more slowly, and your breathing becomes deeper.
3. In the first part of sleep the muscles relax. It is not a very deep sleep.
4. Part two of sleep happens about 30 minutes later. The sleeper falls into a deeper rest.
5. In part three the body becomes more relaxed, and blood pressure drops.
6. Part four is the deepest part. It is difficult to wake the sleeper.
7. You dream about four or five times a night, but you probably do not remember all of your dreams.

Pages 34-35. Fables

Part A: 2

Part B: Answers will vary but should include idea that "looks aren't everything."

Pages 36-37. Paraphrasing

Part A: **1.** b **2.** c

Part B: Answers will vary.

Pages 38-39. Alliteration

Part A: **1.** c **2.** b **3.** c **4.** b

Part B: For questions 1-4, answers will vary.

Pages 40-41. Haiku

Part A: For questions 1-6, answers will vary.

Part B: For questions 1-4, answers will vary.

Pages 42-43. Suspense

Part A: 1, 3, 5, and 8

Part B: Answers for questions 1 and 2 will vary.

Pages 44-45. Multiple Word Meaning

Part A: **1.** a **2.** a **3.** b **4.** a **5.** b **6.** b **7.** a **8.** a

Part B: **1.** trip **2.** stick **3.** log **4.** punch **5.** skip **6.** rest **7.** firm **8.** long

Pages 46-47. Probability and Certainty

Part A: **1.** b, c **2.** b, c

Part B: Answers will vary.

Page 48. Imagery in Poetry

Part A: 2, 3, 5, and 8

Part B: Answers for questions 1-6 will vary.

Part C: Answers will vary.